10/05

J977.2
H

Indiana

BY ANN HEINRICHS

Content Adviser: Andrea Bean Hough, M.A., M.L.S., Senior Subject Specialist, Indiana Division, Indiana State Library, Indianapolis, Indiana

Reading Adviser: Dr. Linda D. Labbo, Department of Reading Education, College of Education, The University of Georgia

COMPASS POINT BOOKS MINNEAPOLIS, MINNESOTA

Compass Point Books
3109 West 50th Street, #115
Minneapolis, MN 55410

Visit Compass Point Books on the Internet at *www.compasspointbooks.com*
or e-mail your request to *custserv@compasspointbooks.com*

On the cover: Soldiers and Sailors Monument in Indianapolis

Photographs ©: Unicorn Stock Photos/Andre Jenny, cover, 1, 39; Courtesy of Gary Berdeaux/Cave
Country Adventures, 3, 40; James P. Rowan, 4, 13, 24, 26, 43 (top), 45; Corbis/Layne Kennedy, 6;
Unicorn Stock Photos/Jeff Greenberg, 8, 35; Tom Stack & Associates/Sharon Gerig, 9, 21, 27; Unicorn
Stock Photos/Tom Edwards, 10, 42; Carroll County Historical Society Museum, Delphi, Indiana, 11, 41;
Corbis/David Muench, 12, 38; Courtesy of Angel Mounds State Historic Site, Indiana Department of
Natural Resources, 14, 47; North Wind Picture Archives, 15, 16 (all); Library of Congress, 17, 19, 48
(top); Corbis/Bettmann, 18; Jim Wark/AirPhoto, 20; Courtesy of The Indiana State Senate/Senate
Communications Department, 22; Hulton/Archive by Getty Images, 25, 46; Corbis/Patrick Bennett, 28;
Getty Images/Mike Simons, 29; Tom Stack & Associates/Lynn Gerig, 30; Photo permission, Paws, Inc.
"Garfield" & "Garfield Characters" © Paws, All rights reserved, 31; Getty Images/Christopher Little/
CBS/Online USA, Inc., 32; Getty Images/Matthew Stockman/ALLSPORT, 33; Photo Network/Grace
Davies, 34; Max & Bea Hunn/Image Finders, 36; Robesus, Inc., 43 (state flag); One Mile Up, Inc., 43
(state seal); Robert McCaw, 44 (top); Tom Edwards/Visuals Unlimited, 44 (middle); Artville, 44 (bottom).

Editors: E. Russell Primm, Emily J. Dolbear, and Patricia Stockland
Photo Researcher: Marcie C. Spence
Photo Selector: Linda S. Koutris
Designer/Page Production: The Design Lab/Jaime Martens
Cartographer: XNR Productions, Inc.

Library of Congress Cataloging-in-Publication Data
Heinrichs, Ann.
  Indiana / by Ann Heinrichs.
      p. cm. — (This land is your land)
  Summary: Describes the geography, history, government, people, culture, and attractions of Indiana.
  Includes bibliographical references and index.
    ISBN 0-7565-0325-6 (hardcover : alk. paper)
    1. Indiana—Juvenile literature. [1. Indiana.] I. Title.
    F526.3 .H45 2003
    977.2—dc21   2002153297

Table of Contents

NOTE: In this book, words that are defined in the glossary are in **bold** *the first time they appear in the text.*

▲ The Upper Falls of Mill Creek in Cataract Falls Recreation Area

Comedian David Letterman, singer Michael Jackson, and the cartoon cat Garfield all had their beginnings in Indiana. Many famous authors did, too. One is Kurt Vonnegut Jr., who wrote about growing up in Indiana. There were "millions and millions of acres of topsoil all around us," Vonnegut said, "as flat as pool tables and as rich as chocolate cake."

Indiana's rich, black soil makes it an important farming state. Indiana is also the nation's leading steelmaking state, but it has much more than cornfields and steel mills. Tall sand dunes rise along its lakeshores. Deep forests cover southern Indiana. Beneath them run miles of underground caves.

Indiana's state motto is "The Crossroads of America." Dozens of highway, railroad, and water routes crisscross the state. They make it easy to travel and ship goods to faraway places. They also make it convenient for people to visit. Once you discover more about Indiana, you'll want to visit, too!

▲ Part of northern Indiana faces Lake Michigan.

Indiana is one of America's Midwest states. It's located in the north-central United States. Indiana is also one of the Great Lakes states. A small part of northern Indiana faces Lake Michigan. The state of Michigan forms the rest of Indiana's northern border. To the east is Ohio, and to the west is Illinois. On the south, across the Ohio River, is Kentucky.

Northern Indiana is part of the Great Lakes Plains. Its soil is dark and fertile. Many lakes are found here, too. One is Lake Wawasee, Indiana's largest natural lake.

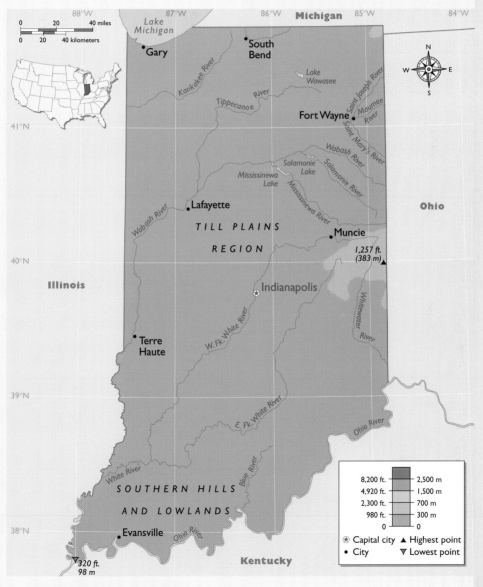

88°W · 87°W · 86°W · Michigan · 85°W · 84°W

Lake Michigan

0   20   40 miles
0   20   40 kilometers

Gary

South Bend

Lake Wawasee

Kankakee River

Tippecanoe River

Saint Joseph River

Fort Wayne

Saint Mary's River

Maumee River

41°N

Wabash River

Salamonie Lake

Salamonie River

Mississinewa Lake

Mississinewa River

Lafayette

TILL PLAINS REGION

Muncie

1,257 ft. (383 m) ▲

40°N

Illinois

Indianapolis

Ohio

W. Fk. White River

Whitewater River

39°N

Terre Haute

E. Fk. White River

Ohio River

White River

Blue River

SOUTHERN HILLS AND LOWLANDS

38°N

Evansville

Ohio River

Kentucky

▽ 320 ft. 98 m

8,200 ft.	2,500 m
4,920 ft.	1,500 m
2,300 ft.	700 m
980 ft.	300 m
0	0

⊛ Capital city   ▲ Highest point
• City   ▽ Lowest point

▲ **A topographic map of Indiana**

Giant sand dunes rise along Lake Michigan. Much of this area is protected as Indiana Dunes National Lakeshore. Many steel plants and other **industries** developed along the lakeshore, too. These industries led to the growth of cities such as Gary, East Chicago, and Michigan City. Water and air pollution often have been problems in these areas.

Central Indiana is called the Till Plains region. These rolling plains are known for their rich soil. They are part of the Corn Belt that stretches across the Midwest. Indiana farmers grow crops and raise livestock in this region.

▲ **Visitors enjoy Indiana Dunes National Lakeshore.**

▲ Turkey Run State Park is located in central Indiana.

South-central Indiana is called the Southern Hills and Low-lands. It's a region of hills and valleys. **Knobs** rise here and there. Vast deposits of **limestone** lie underground, and many streams and cave systems run through the limestone.

▲ A view of the Indianapolis skyline along the White River

Indiana's rivers helped the state develop. The Ohio River has always been an important travel route. It's one of the biggest tributaries, or branches, of the Mississippi River.

The Wabash River forms part of Indiana's border with Illinois. Its waters join the Ohio River. The White and Tippecanoe Rivers are the Wabash's major tributaries. Indianapolis, the state capital, lies along the White River.

The Saint Joseph and Saint Mary's Rivers meet at Fort Wayne. There they join to form the Maumee River. The Maumee then runs northeast toward Lake Erie. Indianans completed the Wabash and Erie **Canal** in 1853. It joined the Maumee River with the Ohio River and allowed people to ship goods from the Great Lakes to the Mississippi River.

▲ **The Wabash and Erie Canal**

▲ Sulphur Pond in Hoosier National Forest

Forests once covered almost all of Indiana. Today, most of these forests are in the southern part of the state. That's where Hoosier National Forest is located. Deer and red foxes still make their homes in the forests. Some of the smaller animals that live there are muskrats, chipmunks, gophers, and squirrels.

Quail, pheasant, and grouse live in the forests and fields. Hundreds of species of birds pass through in the spring and fall. Many of them feed among the **marshes** of the Indiana Dunes.

Indiana gets cold winters and hot summers. Winters are much colder in the northern part of the state than in the southern part. Snowfall is heavier near Lake Michigan, too. It's caused by cold air passing over the warm lake. This is called lake-effect snow. In the summer, however, the lake helps keep the north cool. Summers in southern Indiana can be quite hot.

Tornado time in Indiana is in spring and summer. The state is part of the Midwest's "tornado belt." In 1990, forty-nine tornadoes struck Indiana, the most ever in one year.

▲ Hiking on a snowy winter day in Indiana Dunes State Park

A Trip Through Time

People called the Mound Builders once lived in Indiana. They settled in the Ohio River Valley about 2,500 years ago. They built huge, flat-topped mounds of earth. Some mounds were burial sites. Others were bases for temples or homes.

▲ These reconstructed huts at the Angel Mounds State Historic Site in Evansville are similar to the homes the Mound Builders lived in thousands of years ago.

Later, many Native American groups began moving in. Several tribes in northern Indiana formed the Miami Confederation. The Miami raised corn in the summer. They hunted bison, or buffalo, in the winter. More Native American groups arrived as white settlers pushed westward. They included the Kickapoo, Potawatomi, Wyandot, Shawnee, and Delaware.

René-Robert Cavelier, Sieur de La Salle, was the first European in Indiana. He was a French explorer from Canada. La Salle crossed northern Indiana in 1679. Around 1732, the French built a fort at Vincennes. This was Indiana's first permanent settlement. Great Britain won the region from France in 1763.

▲ René-Robert Cavelier, Sieur de La Salle

▲ General George Rogers Clark (left) leading his troops across the Wabash River in 1779

▲ Chief Tecumseh and General William Henry Harrison confront each other.

The British were not very interested in Indiana. They made a lot of money from their thirteen **colonies** to the east. The **colonists,** however, wanted freedom from Britain and fought the British in the Revolutionary War (1775–1783). In 1779, the war reached Indiana with the Battle of Vincennes. General George Rogers Clark led American troops in this conflict and defeated the British. Indiana became part of the Northwest Territory after the war.

In 1800, Indiana Territory was created. As more settlers poured in, Native Americans fought to keep their lands. Shawnee chief Tecumseh united several tribes to resist the settlers. General William

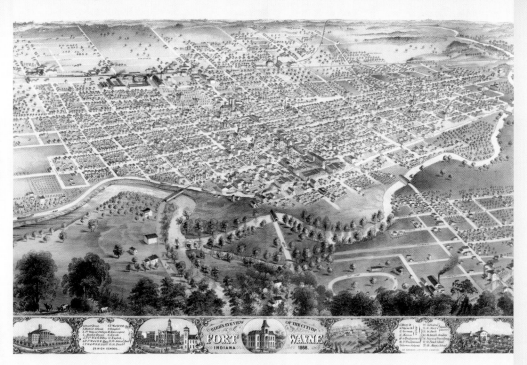

▲ A drawing of Fort Wayne in 1868 shows the path of one of many new canals crossing the state.

Henry Harrison led U.S. troops to fight the Native Americans. Harrison's men defeated these unified tribes at the Battle of Tippecanoe near Lafayette in 1811.

Indiana became the nation's nineteenth state in 1816. The **National Road** reached Indiana in 1830. Settlers from eastern states traveled the road to Indiana, which they knew was a good state for farming. Indiana became a leading source of corn, wheat, and hogs. By the 1850s, new canals and railroads crossed the state. This made it easier for farmers to ship their goods to market.

Meanwhile, the issue of slavery was tearing the nation apart. Like other Northerners, most Indianans were against slavery. Some residents took part in the Underground Railroad. This secret network helped Southern slaves escape to freedom. Levi and Katie Coffin of Fountain City helped more than two thousand runaway slaves. Slavery finally came to an end after the Civil War (1861–1865).

A big industrial boom began in the late 1800s. The Standard Oil company built a huge oil-refining plant in Whiting.

▲ Studebaker automobiles outside the home of manufacturer J. M. Studebaker in 1908

▲ **Workers in Hammond inspecting and painting bomb shells in 1942**

Inland Steel opened a steel plant in East Chicago. Next, the U.S. Steel company built massive steel mills in Gary. Dozens of other oil and steel plants followed. In South Bend, the Studebaker brothers began making cars. Thousands of **immigrants** poured into Indiana in search of jobs.

Indiana's industries were busier than ever during World War II (1939–1945). Indiana factories made airplanes, tanks, guns, and other war supplies. After the war, the state's factories continued to grow. At the same time, farm machines were replacing farmworkers. Thousands of people left their farms for factory jobs.

▲ An overhead view of a blast furnace in Gary and the raw materials used to make iron

During the 1960s, Americans began buying more foreign-made cars. As a result, Indiana's automobile industry suffered. Foreign-made steel hurt the state's steel industry in the 1980s, too. Fortunately, both industries improved by the 1990s. State leaders, however, continue to work to bring new industries to Indiana.

Government by the People

▲ Fountains outside the state capitol in Indianapolis

Indiana has had three capital cities. Vincennes was the capital of Indiana Territory. Corydon served as the capital from 1813 to 1825. Indianapolis became the capital in 1825.

Like the U.S. government, Indiana's state government has three branches—legislative, executive, and judicial. Each branch has a special job to do.

The legislative branch makes the state laws. These laws

cover many areas of daily life, ranging from taxes to public schools to pet licenses. Voters elect lawmakers to serve in Indiana's General Assembly. It has two chambers, or houses. They are the 50-member senate and the 100-member house of representatives.

The executive branch makes sure the state's laws are carried out. Indiana's governor is the head of the executive branch. Voters choose a governor every four years. The governor can serve only two terms in a row. Also, a governor can serve only two terms in any twelve-year period. Voters elect seven

▲ The Indiana State Senate Chamber, where senators meet when the General Assembly is in session

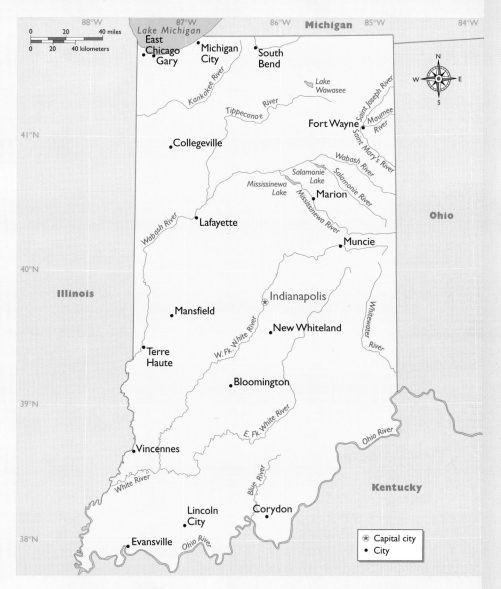

▲ **A geopolitical map of Indiana**

other executive officers, as well. These include the treasurer
and the superintendent of public instruction. The governor
appoints people to head many state departments and agencies.

▲ **The Lake County Courthouse in Crown Point**

The judicial branch is made up of judges and their courts. The judges and juries decide whether a person or company has broken the law. Indiana's highest court is the Indiana Supreme Court. It has five justices, or judges. The governor appoints them for their first term. After that, voters can decide if a judge should continue serving.

Indiana is divided into ninety-two counties. Most are

governed by a three-member board of commissioners. Marion County and the city of Indianapolis have a joint government. Indiana also has cities, towns, and townships. Cities elect a mayor and city council. Most towns elect a town council. The township trustee is the main official in a township.

Two U.S. presidents have come from Indiana. One is William Henry Harrison, the ninth U.S. president (1841). Harrison was born in Virginia and later lived in Indiana. He died after only one month in office. The other is his grandson, Benjamin Harrison. He served as the twenty-third U.S. president (1889–1893). Indiana has also produced five U.S. vice presidents.

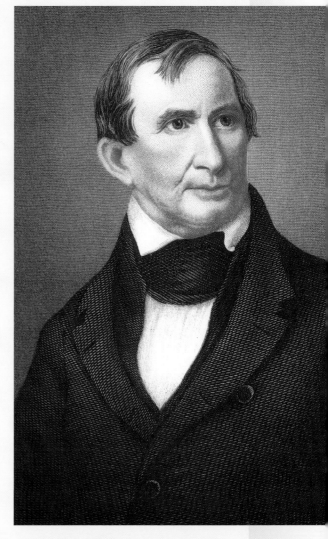

▲ Indianan William Henry Harrison was the ninth president of the United States.

▲ A cornfield in Parke County

Travel across Indiana, and you'll see acres of farmland. Indiana is one of America's best farming states. It ranks among the top five in the nation for corn, soybeans, hogs, chickens, and eggs. Indiana grows almost one out of every ten bushels of America's corn and soybeans.

Indiana farmers raise dozens of other crops, too. These include tomatoes, snap beans, cucumbers, hay, cantaloupes, and watermelons. Herbs such as peppermint and spearmint also grow in Indiana.

Hogs are the state's most valuable farm animal. Many farmers raise chickens, dairy cattle, and beef cattle. Some of the dairy cows' milk is made into ice cream! Only California produces more ice cream than Indiana.

Ice cream is also one of Indiana's many factory products. The state's top factory goods are actually transportation equipment. This includes cars, trucks, buses, motor homes, railroad cars, and airplanes. Some factories make the parts, while others put the parts together.

▲ **Beef cattle in Lawrence County**

▲ **This bus factory is located in Mitchell.**

Chemicals are important Indiana products, too. You may not think of medicines as chemicals, but they are. Medicines and drugs are Indiana's leading chemical products. Eli Lilly in Indianapolis is one of America's top drug companies.

No other state makes more steel than Indiana. The tall smokestacks of steel mills rise throughout the Calumet region. That's an area of northwest Indiana along Lake Michigan. Indiana factories also produce aluminum and process petroleum. Other states, however, provide the raw materials for most of these products. The major mining products in Indiana are coal, limestone, sand, and gravel.

Until the 1950s, farming was Indiana's leading industry. Then manufacturing took its place. Today, more than three out of every four Indiana workers hold a service job. Service workers are found everywhere in the community. Some work in stores, hospitals, banks, or repair shops. Others teach school, drive trucks, or build houses. They all have special skills that make life better for both residents and visitors.

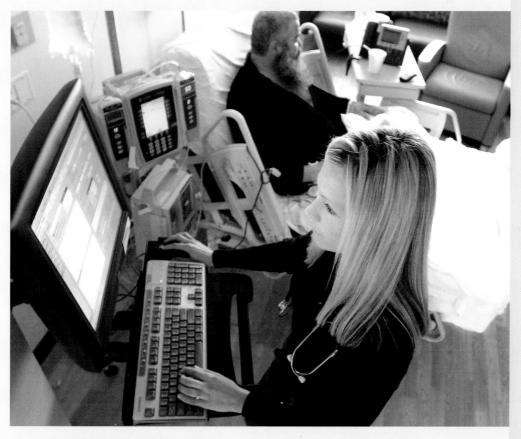

▲ This nurse at Indiana Heart Hospital is one of many service workers in Indiana who make life better for its residents.

▲ **An Amish woman uses horse-drawn farm equipment to cut oats in Allen County.**

Indiana had 6,080,485 residents in 2000. About seven out of every eight Indianans are white. Their ancestors came from England, Scotland, Ireland, Germany, Poland, Hungary, or Italy. Several communities of Amish people live in the northeast. This religious group follows a simple way of life that relies heavily on farming.

Gary, East Chicago, and Indianapolis have large African-American populations. **Hispanic,** Asian, and Native American people live in the state, too.

The people of Indiana are called Hoosiers—but why? No one knows for sure. Some people say the name comes from Indiana's **pioneer** days. When someone knocked on the door, pioneers would holler, "Who's yere?" The question sounded like Hoosier.

Some say the word comes from "hushers." They were Indianans who got in a lot of fights. They could "hush" their enemies by beating them up. However it got its start, the name *Hoosiers* is part of American **folklore.**

Have you ever seen the comic-strip cat named Garfield? Garfield is lazy, eats lasagna, and has a sassy attitude. He was created by Jim Davis of Marion. Jim grew up on a farm with twenty-five cats. He's just one of many artists, writers, and entertainers from Indiana.

▲ **Odie the dog and Garfield the cat with their creator, Jim Davis**

▲ Comedian David Letterman hosts a
late night talk show.

Comedians David Letterman and Red Skelton came from Indiana. Actors Shelley Long, James Dean, and Florence Henderson did, too. Songwriters Cole Porter and Hoagy Carmichael and singer Michael Jackson are all from Indiana. Other famous Indianans include poet James Whitcomb Riley and mystery writer Rex Stout.

The Indianapolis 500 is Indiana's most famous event. This car race takes place on Memorial Day weekend, at the end of May. Another Memorial Day event is the Spirit of Vincennes Rendezvous. Costumed soldiers there act out George Rogers Clark's Revolutionary War victory.

Indianans celebrate many other festivals. There's a Tulipfest in Bloomington and a Mushroom Festival in Mansfield. At the Marion Easter Pageant, performers act out the historic events leading to Easter. South Bend holds its Summer in the City Festival in June. The Three Rivers Festival is a ten-day fair in Fort Wayne.

When basketball season arrives, Indianans go wild. No other state gets quite as excited about its high school basketball teams. As a result, tournament time in Indiana is called Hoosier **Hysteria.**

Larry Bird was a basketball star who played for Indiana State University and the Boston Celtics. He became a member of the Basketball Hall of Fame in 1998. As a coach, Bird led the Indiana Pacers to the National Basketball Association (NBA) finals in 2000. Basketball fans also

▲ The Indianapolis 500 is a famous car race that takes place at the Indianapolis Motor Speedway.

cheer for the Fever of the Women's National Basketball Association (WNBA). The Indianapolis Colts entertain the state's football fans.

The University of Notre Dame is located near South Bend. It's one of the top Roman Catholic universities in the country. Notre Dame's Fighting Irish football team is one of the country's best. Indiana University (IU) and Purdue University are considered top-notch universities, too. IU's basketball team, the Indiana Hoosiers, has won five national championships.

▲ **Sacred Heart Church at the University of Notre Dame**

▲ Actors in costume re-create pioneer life in Conner Prairie.

You'll find much more than sand dunes at Indiana Dunes State Park. Its sandy beaches stretch for miles. Farther inland, thick forests cover the dunes. Deer and coyotes roam there, and hundreds of species of birds flit through the trees. Tall cattails stand in the marshes, and long-legged herons wade nearby.

You'll see pioneer days come to life at Conner Prairie, a living history museum near Fishers. Its "citizens" are weavers, woodworkers, blacksmiths, and other craftspeople. They tell about what daily life was like during the 1830s. At the museum's

Delaware Indian village, visitors can take part in grinding corn and building **dugout** canoes.

Settlers built New Harmony as an ideal community during the 1800s. They believed in equality and freedom of thought. People still visit this village to recall the Harmonists' values. Its shrubbery maze challenges their minds, too. For Harmonists, it stood for the difficult path to "true harmony."

▲ **Log cabins in New Harmony**

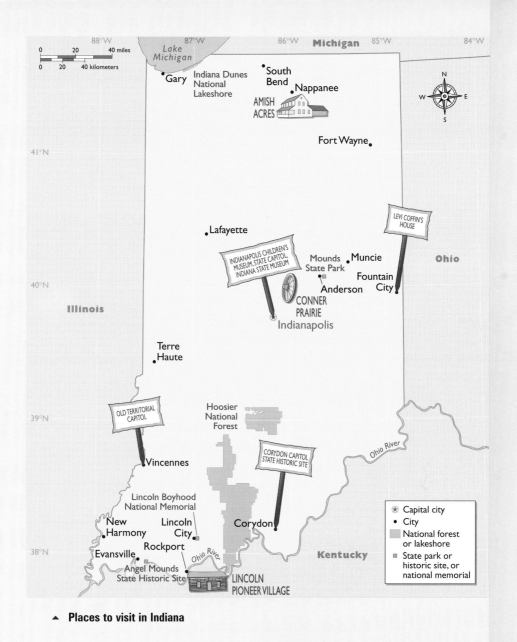

▲ **Places to visit in Indiana**

What was life like in Abraham Lincoln's time? You'll find out at Lincoln Pioneer Village in Rockport. Its log cabins, schools, and churches recall life as Lincoln saw it. The

Lincoln Boyhood National Memorial is located in Lincoln City. It's the site of the cabin where Lincoln grew up.

Levi Coffin shared Lincoln's vision of freedom for slaves. Coffin's house still stands in Fountain City. There you can see how the Coffins hid escaped slaves.

Amish Acres is in Nappanee. Here you can ride a farm wagon and learn about the Amish. You can also sample Amish crafts and foods and watch a play about Amish life.

Mounds State Park near Anderson preserves early Native Americans' earthen mounds. Many earthen structures also remain at Angel Mounds near Evansville.

Would you like to meet SuperCroc? It was the biggest crocodile that ever lived and was so enormous that it ate dinosaurs for dinner! SuperCroc

▲ A log cabin at the Lincoln Boyhood National Memorial

▲ The Children's Museum in Indianapolis

is just one of the many exciting exhibits at Indianapolis's
Children's Museum. While you're in town, visit the beautiful
state capitol. If the lawmakers are meeting, you're welcome
to watch them work. Nearby is the Indiana State Museum. Its
exhibits include a Mound Builders' village.

Corydon was Indiana's first state capital. Its government
building is preserved as a historic site. Vincennes, the first
territorial capital, also preserves its historical buildings.

Wyandotte Cave has several miles of underground passages. It's one of the largest caves in North America. Take a tour, and you'll see awesome rock formations. You may also catch a glimpse of rare Indiana bats.

▲ The Pillar of Constitution is one of the many interesting rock formations in Wyandotte Cave.

You'll get a great view of Hoosier National Forest from Hickory Ridge Lookout Tower. Hemlock Cliffs is a peaceful spot, with waterfalls tumbling beside rushing streams.

Five areas in Hoosier National Forest are called Watchable Wildlife sites. Creep along quietly, and who knows what you might see? You may catch a glimpse of deer, foxes, woodchucks, opossums, or wild turkeys. If you sit still and simply enjoy the nature around you, it's easy to imagine Indiana's past and see its great future.

Important Dates

1679 French explorer René-Robert Cavelier, Sieur de La Salle, becomes the first European to reach Indiana.

1732 French settlers found Vincennes, the first permanent settlement in Indiana.

1763 Indiana passes from France to Great Britain.

1800 Indiana Territory is established.

1811 William Henry Harrison defeats Native Americans at the Battle of Tippecanoe.

1816 Indiana becomes the nineteenth U.S. state on December 11.

1825 Indianapolis becomes Indiana's capital.

1841 William Henry Harrison becomes the ninth U.S. president.

1853 The Wabash and Erie Canal is completed, linking Fort Wayne on the Maumee River and Evansville on the Ohio River.

1889 Benjamin Harrison becomes the twenty-third U.S. president.

1906 The United States Steel Corporation begins building its steel plant in Gary.

1911 The first Indianapolis 500 car races are held.

1937 The Ohio River floods, causing many deaths and widespread damage.

1966 Indiana Dunes National Lakeshore is established.

1987 The Pan-American Games are held in Indianapolis.

1989 Dan Quayle of Indiana becomes the U.S. vice president under George H. W. Bush.

2000 The Indiana Pacers reach the National Basketball Association (NBA) finals.

2002 Indiana astronaut David Wolf completes his third mission in space.

Glossary

canal—a human-made waterway

colonies—territories that belong to the countries that settle them

colonists—people who settle a new land for their home country

dugout—a boat made by hollowing out a large log

folklore—tales, sayings, and customs among a group of people

Hispanic—people of Mexican, South American, and other Spanish-speaking cultures

hysteria—a state of extreme emotional excitement

immigrants—people who come to another country to live permanently

industries—businesses or trades

knobs—steep hills

limestone—hard rock that contains calcium

marshes—wetlands

National Road—an overland route established in 1803 from Maryland to Illinois, which was eventually overshadowed by the railroads

pioneer—someone who explores or settles in a new land

Did You Know?

★ The name *Indiana* means "Land of the Indians."

★ Abraham Lincoln lived in Indiana from age seven through age twenty-one. His homesite in Spencer County is now named Lincoln City.

★ Mark Spitz of Indiana University won seven gold medals for swimming in the 1972 Olympic Games. No other athlete has won that many gold medals in a single set of Olympic games.

★ Twelve stagecoach lines once ran through Indiana on the National Road. That road is now Interstate 40.

★ More major highways run through Indianapolis than any other city in America.

State capital: Indianapolis

State motto: The Crossroads of America

Popular nickname: Hoosier State

Statehood: December 11, 1816; nineteenth state

Land area: 35,870 square miles (92,903 sq km); **rank:** thirty-eighth

Highest point: Franklin Township, Wayne County, 1,257 feet (383 m) above sea level

Lowest point: Posey County on the Ohio River, 320 feet (98 m) above sea level

Highest recorded temperature: 116°F (47°C) at Collegeville on July 14, 1936

Lowest recorded temperature: −36°F (−38°C) at New Whiteland on January 19, 1994

Average January temperature: 28°F (−2°C)

Average July temperature: 75°F (24°C)

Population in 2000: 6,080,485; **rank:** fourteenth

Largest cities in 2000: Indianapolis (791,926), Fort Wayne (205,727), Evansville (121,582), South Bend (107,789)

Factory products: Transportation equipment, chemicals, metals and metal goods

Farm products: Corn, soybeans, hogs, chickens, dairy and beef cattle

Mining products: Coal, limestone, sand, gravel

State flag: Indiana's state flag shows a flaming gold torch against a field of blue. The torch stands for freedom and the light of wisdom and knowledge. Nineteen gold stars surround the torch. The thirteen outer stars stand for the first thirteen states. The five stars of the inner circle stand for the next five states to join the Union before Indiana. The large nineteenth star above the torch stands for how Indiana became the nineteenth state in the Union. Above that star is the word *Indiana*.

State seal: The state seal shows a scene of Indiana's pioneer days. It includes a woodcutter with his ax in the forest and a bison, or buffalo, jumping over a log. In the background, the sun sets behind a row of mountains. That is a symbol of the pioneers' urge to move westward. This westward movement led to the exploration and settlement of Indiana. At the bottom of the seal is "1816," the date of Indiana's statehood.

State abbreviations: Ind. (traditional); IN (postal)

State Symbols

State bird: Cardinal

State flower: Peony

State tree: Tulip tree (yellow poplar)

State stone: Salem limestone

State river: Wabash River

State poem: "Indiana," by Arthur Franklin Mapes

State commemorative quarter: Released on December 11, 2002

Making Cornmeal Muffins

Muffins are among the many delicious foods made from Indiana's corn crops. Makes about twelve muffins.

INGREDIENTS:

1 cup cornmeal

1 cup flour

2 tablespoons sugar

4 teaspoons baking powder

½ teaspoon salt

1 large egg

¼ cup vegetable oil

1 cup milk

DIRECTIONS:

Make sure an adult helps you with the hot oven. Preheat the oven to 400°F. Grease a muffin tin. In a large bowl, mix together the cornmeal, flour, sugar, baking powder, and salt. In a different bowl, beat the egg, and then add the oil and milk. Gently blend the wet ingredients into the dry ones. Spoon this mixture into the muffin tin. Fill each cup a little more than half full. Bake until golden brown—about 18 to 20 minutes.

"On the Banks of the Wabash, Far Away"

Words and music by Paul Dresser

'Round my Indiana homestead wave the
cornfields,
In the distance loom the woodlands clear
and cool.
Oftentimes my thoughts revert to scenes
of childhood,
Where I first received my lessons, nature's
school.
But one thing there is missing in the picture,
Without her face it seems so incomplete.
I long to see my mother in the doorway,
As she stood there years ago, her boy
to greet.

Chorus:
Oh, the moonlight's fair tonight along the
Wabash,
From the fields there comes the breath of
new mown hay.
Through the sycamores the candle lights
are gleaming,
On the banks of the Wabash, far away.

Many years have passed since I strolled
by the river,
Arm in arm, with sweetheart Mary by
my side,
It was there I tried to tell her that I loved
her,
It was there I begged of her to be my bride.
Long years have passed since I strolled
thro' the churchyard.
She's sleeping there, my angel, Mary dear,
I loved her, but she thought I didn't mean it,
Still I'd give my future were she only here.

Famous Indianans

Larry Bird (1956–) was a basketball star with Indiana State University and the Boston Celtics. He later coached the Indiana Pacers.

Hoagy Carmichael (1899–1981) was a singer and songwriter. He was born in Bloomington.

Jim Davis (1945–) is a cartoonist from Marion. He created the comic strip "Garfield."

James Dean (1931–1955) was an actor. *Rebel Without a Cause* (1955) was his most famous movie. Dean was born in Marion.

Benjamin Harrison (1833–1901) was the twenty-third U.S. president (1889–1893). He had a home in Indianapolis. Born in Ohio, he was the grandson of William Henry Harrison.

William Henry Harrison (1773–1841) was the Indiana Territory's first governor (1800–1812). Harrison (pictured above left) defeated the Native Americans in the Battle of Tippecanoe (1811) and later became the ninth U.S. president (1841). He was born in Virginia.

Florence Henderson (1934–) is an actress. She is best known as the mother on television's *The Brady Bunch.* Henderson was born in Dale.

Michael Jackson (1958–) is a popular singer, dancer, and songwriter. He was born in Gary.

David Letterman (1947–) is a comedian and talk-show host from Indianapolis. He hosts *The Late Show* on television.

Shelley Long (1949–) is an actress from Fort Wayne. She is best known for playing Diane in the television comedy *Cheers.*

Cole Porter (1891–1964) wrote many popular songs for musical theater from the 1930s through the 1950s. Porter was born in Peru.

Dan Quayle (1947–) was the U.S. vice president under George H. W. Bush (1989–1993). Quayle was born in Indianapolis.

James Whitcomb Riley (1849–1916) was known as the Hoosier Poet. His poems include "Little Orphant Annie" and "When the Frost Is on the Punkin." Riley was born in Greenfield.

Red Skelton (1913–1997) was a comedian. He created zany characters such as Clem Kadiddlehopper. Skelton was born in Vincennes.

Rex Stout (1886–1975) wrote mystery stories with detective Nero Wolfe as the hero. He was born in Noblesville.

Twyla Tharp (1941–) is a dancer and choreographer. She was born in Portland.

Kurt Vonnegut Jr. (1922–) writes science-fiction novels with wild plots and a dark brand of humor. He was born in Indianapolis.

Want to Know More?

At the Library

Butler, Dori Hillestad, and Eileen Potts Dawson. *H is for Hoosier.* Black Earth, Wis.: Trail Books, 2001.

Chambers, Catherine E., and John Lawn (illustrator). *Indiana Days: Life in a Frontier Town.* Mahwah, N.J.: Troll Associates, 1984.

Ling, Bettina. *Indiana.* Danbury, Conn.: Children's Press, 2003.

McKenna, A. T. *Indy Racing.* Edina, Minn.: Abdo & Daughters, 1998.

Rambeck, Richard. *Indiana Pacers.* Mankato, Minn.: Creative Education, 1997.

Stratton-Porter, Gene. *Laddie: A True Blue Story.* Wheaton, Ill.: Tyndale House, 1991.

Teale, Edwin Way. *Dune Boy: The Early Years of a Naturalist.* Storrs, Conn.: Bibliopola Press, 2001.

Waters, Kate, and Marjory Dressler (photographer). *The Mysterious Horseman: An Adventure in Prairietown, 1836.* New York: Scholastic, 1994.

Welsbacher, Anne. *Indiana.* Edina, Minn.: Abdo & Daughters, 1998.

On the Web

AccessIndiana

http://www.in.gov

To learn about Indiana's history, government, economy, and land

Enjoy Indiana

http://www.enjoyindiana.com

To find out about Indiana's events, activities, and sights

Indiana Historical Society

http://www.indianahistory.org

For information about Indiana's history

Through the Mail

Indiana Department of Commerce

Tourism Division
One North Capitol Avenue, Suite 700
Indianapolis, IN 46204

For information on travel and interesting sights in Indiana

Indiana State Information Center

Department of Administration
402 West Washington Street, Room W160A
Indianapolis, IN 46204

For information on Indiana's government services

On the Road

Indiana State House

West Washington Street
and Capitol Avenue
Indianapolis, IN 46204
317/233-5293

To visit Indiana's state capitol

Index

About the Author

Ann Heinrichs grew up in Fort Smith, Arkansas, and lives in Chicago. She is the author of more than one hundred books for children and young adults on Asian, African, and U.S. history and culture. Ann has also written numerous newspaper, magazine, and encyclopedia articles. She is an award-winning martial artist, specializing in t'ai chi empty-hand and sword forms.

Ann has traveled widely throughout the United States, Africa, Asia, and the Middle East. In exploring each state for this series, she rediscovered the people, history, and resources that make this a great land, as well as the concerns we share with people around the world.